Improv Games for One Player

Improv Games for One Player

A Very Concise Collection of Musical Games for

One Classical Musician

Volume 1

Jeffrey Agrell

GIA Publications, Inc.
Chicago

Improv Games for One Player
Jeffrey Agrell

G-7747
ISBN: 978-1-57999-792-2

Copyright © 2010 GIA Publications, Inc.
7404 S Mason Ave
Chicago IL 60638

www.giamusic.com

Contents

1
Introduction

What

My *Improvisation Games for Classical Musicians* (GIA, G-7173) is a wonderful and comprehensive resource; but the vast content of that volume does not fit comfortably into the average musician's instrument case. *Improv Games for One Player* is a more slender book of non-jazz musical games that is utterly portable. It should fit in just about every case with enough room to transport a sheet of music paper, but still contains plenty of content to enliven and enrich a player's daily technical and musical practice for a long time. About half of this material is drawn from the original big book, and half from new, previously unpublished material collected and invented by me.

Why

Why improvise? To have fun, to further technique and musicianship, and to acquire fluency and flexibility (to be ready for anything musically that comes along). It's all well and good to play standard etudes and technical exercises, but to really achieve comprehensive musicianship, you need to improvise. After you get into it, you will discover that improvisation is a terrific learning tool, not to mention being more fun than is probably legal in some states. It's also a great feeling to rejoin this age-old tradition, which was lost from every musician's training beginning around the middle of the nineteenth century to the present day. There are, however, promising signs that the tradition of improvisation is reviving among the most progressive classical musicians.

Who

All instrumentalists and vocalists. Everybody. No experience in improvisation necessary!

When

Now. Every day. As much as possible.

How

1. Open book.
2. Get idea.
3. Close book.
4. Play. And play. And play.

Then What?

Enlist your best friends on any instrument to get in on the fun. Work separately using *Improv Games for One Player*. Then pick up the big book mentioned above and start making improvised chamber music. Give concerts! Teach others! The sky's the limit in this new-old incredibly fun and interesting field of spontaneous classical music creation.

2
Warm-up Game

Warm-up Interval Piece

This is an application of long-tone warm-ups. Choose two to four intervals and use them to make up a slow piece. This game is very good for one player alone, but can be done with two, three, or even four players at once, who may agree on the same variation (listed below) or select independently.

Suggestions

1. Vary the number of beats (quarter note = 60) of each long tone from 2 to 9 (or more) beats.
2. Don't forget to invest your music with some emotion—add some heartfelt dynamics, crescendos and decrescendos, and silences.
3. You may discontinue a line at any point, rest, and then begin anew some distance away. For example, your line leads you to the top of the staff, where you hold it out, rest for 4 beats, then begin again on middle C.
4. All of the variations below may use whole and/or half steps occasionally as transitions between the main interval(s).

Variations

1. **Atonal 1**
   Major or minor sevenths and tritones
2. **Atonal 2**
   Fourths and tritones
3. **Atonal 3**
   Minor ninth (flat nine) and tritone
4. **Heroic**
   Fourths and fifths
5. **Dolce**
   Major thirds
6. **Romantic**
   Major and minor sixths
7. **Dark**
   Minor thirds
8. **Custom**
   Pick a unique combination of intervals.
   Examples:
   a. Minc.   jor seventh
   b. Minor seconds and fourths
   c. Major third and minor seventh
9. **The Whole Nine Yards**
   Free choice of any and/or all intervals
10. **Diatonic**
    Free choice of intervals, but choose them from an agreed-upon key.
11. **Wide**
    Free choice of intervals no smaller than a minor sixth
12. **Narrow**
    Use only whole or half steps

3
Rhythm Games

Offbeat Metronome
When practicing scales or any other technical material, *hear* the metronome click on beats two and four instead of on one and three.

Poet Lariat
Use any poem or famous oration as a source of rhythm for an improvisation. Simply play the rhythmic meter of the poem. Keep pitch choices narrow at first; a pentatonic scale would work well here.

Swing It
Take any technical exercise (scale, arpeggio, pattern), etude, familiar tune (folk song, camp song, pop tune), classical theme, or melody, or just make it up—and play all the eighth notes swing style. If you don't know what swing is, "it don't mean a thing"; just go and listen (and sing along) to a lot of big band music from the 30s and 40s until the concept of swing (swung eighth notes) becomes clear.

Transformation
Transform any familiar tune using a different meter (and perhaps a style). For example, play *The Stars and Stripes Forever* as a waltz. Play *Yankee Doodle* in 5/8, or *America, the Beautiful* in 7/8.

4
Accent Game

Scale Accents

When practicing daily scales and arpeggios, add various accent patterns (accent every other note, every third note, or every fourth note). For a challenge, accent every fifth note or more. The most interesting are those that do not coincide with the meter (ternary accents in duple meter or vice-versa).

More ideas

1. Combine odd and even accent groups. Examples:
   a. 2 + 3
   b. 3 + 2
   c. 3 + 3 + 2
   d. 2 + 2 + 3
   e. 3 + 2 + 2
2. Irregular accents. Improvise accent groupings as you go up and down the scale. Group sometimes in duple, sometimes in triple, sometimes using long groupings.
3. Combine accent groupings with various articulations. Examples:
   a. All staccato
   b. All legato
   c. Combinations of legato and staccato within accent groupings
4. Double the fun and make it a duet. Share a pulse. Try playing exactly the same accent/ articulation patterns as your partner as well as independently choosing accent groupings.

5
Melody Games

Step/Skip: The Pentatonic 24

1. Pick a key and improvise interesting melodies using the pentatonic major scale (scale degrees 1—2—3—5—6; in C: C—D—E—G—A).
2. You may move only to the next adjacent tone in this scale, but you may also at any moment suddenly take a dramatic leap to a tone some distance away.
3. You may, of course, choose to enhance your melody with rests, repeated tones, and variations in articulation, dynamics, rhythms, and timbre.
4. Tomorrow, repeat in a new key.
5. In twelve days you will have played all keys.
6. Begin anew using the pentatonic minor scale (scale degrees 1—2—♭3—5—♭7) for an additional twelve days.

Variation 1

After twenty-four days are up, you may choose to repeat the entire cycle, or repeat using a new scale (major, any kind of minor, a modal scale (Lydian, etc.), the whole-tone scale, a diminished (octotonic) scale (two types: whole/half or half/whole), Blues scale, Klezmer, etc.).

Variation 2

1. Do this ga~~me~~ ~~with a par~~tner.
2. One plays ~~an accompanime~~nt, the other solos.
3. After both have soloed, add a section where you both do both, switching freely on the fly.
4. Steal each other's rhythmic motives and melodic shapes shamelessly.

Rainbow Scales

Play any one-octave scale up and down (only!), but instead of playing it the usual colorless way of using straight eighth notes, add all kinds of variation, changing:

1. Note values
2. Accents
3. Dynamics
4. Articulations
5. Tempo

Add rests. In short: make *music* out of it. Play the line as musically and interestingly (is that a word?) as possible.

Variation

Do the same with two players, playing either independently or relating to each other in some way (one player may lead and the other imitates, mirrors, or matches style; or both intermittently lead and follow).

Far Out

1. Improvise an atonal melody.
2. Emphasize dissonant intervals such major and minor seconds, tritones, and major and minor sevenths.
3. Give the melody coherence by using repetition, sequence, and dynamic phrasing.
4. Extra credit for making an atonal melody irresistibly sensuous, lyrical, and romantic.

How Dry I Am Melodies

Some say that the most popular notes with which to begin a melody have historically been [here in C major] G3—C4—D4—E4, or the opening notes of the old song, *How Dry I Am*.

1. Create as many different melodies as you can that grow out of these notes.
2. Feel free to change rhythms, double one or more of the notes, add rests, etc.
3. Try a variety of keys.
4. See also Fourth Beginning below.

Fourth Beginning

1. There is only rule in this game: begin with the interval of an ascending perfect fourth (as in *Here Comes the Bride*), then continue with one phrase of melody in a distinct style (march, fanfare, declamation, hunting music, elegy, love song, funeral march, bugle call, serenade, pop song, swing tune, and so on).
2. Vary the key each time as well.
3. Repeat repeatedly, trying to make each time different from the last.

Variation 1

Use a *descending* fourth as the beginning interval.

Variation 2

Try a different first interval, either ascending or descending (perfect fifth, major third, etc.).

Variation 3

Make the melodies longer, going even as far as constructing a whole piece.

6
Harmony Games

Familiar Tune

This game has so many musical vitamins and minerals that it should be done daily, but the best reason to do it is because it is both challenging and fun.

1. Choose a familiar tune, something that you already *very* well (a children's song, folk song, Christmas carol, etc.) and try to play it by ear. See the Resources section in the back of this book for a list of Familiar Tunes.

2. Do this in an easy key (C major), then gradually try it in all keys until they are *all* easy keys.

Variation

Begin again and switch modes (playing the tune in minor or in major if the tune was minor). For the daring: add dissonant notes to the harmony.

Minor Attraction

1. Play several familiar minor-mode tunes by ear, one after another.

2. Play them exclusively in C minor.

3. Repeat tomorrow in F minor and the next day in B♭ minor.

4. Move around the circle of fifths through the minor keys of E♭, A♭, C♯, F♯, B, E, A, D, and G.

5. You may choose to add days to the least familiar scales, as many as you need to upgrade your familiarity in the ... approximately that of your most familiar key.

6. You may also construct your own path through the keys, perhaps arranging them (after C minor) in the order of the least familiar first (F♯ minor, A♭ minor, B♭ minor, etc.) or in the order of the most familiar first (A minor, D minor, G minor, etc.).

Here's a list of familiar tunes to get you started. Feel free to add your own and to play them in any order (in fact, change the order every time):

*   *All the Things You Are*
*   *Angel Eyes*
*   *Autumn Leaves*
*   *Blue Bossa*
*   *California Dreamin'*
*   *Dies Irae*
*   *Drill, Ye Tarriers*
*   *Eleanor Rigby*
*   *The Erie Canal*
*   *Follow the Drinking Gourd*

- *Funeral March (Chopin)*
- *Für Elise*
- *Go Down, Moses*
- *God Rest You Merry, Gentlemen*
- *Greensleeves*
- *Habanera (from Carmen)*
- *The Hall of the Mountain King*
- *Heigh Ho*
- *Hit the Road, Jack*
- *It Don't Mean a Thing…*
- *Joshua Fit the Battle of Jericho*
- *The Look of Love*
- *Moscow Nights*
- *My Favorite Things*
- *My Funny Valentine*
- *O Come, Emmanuel*
- *St. James Infirmary*
- *Scarborough Fair*

- *Shadow of Your Smile*
- *Sometimes I Feel Like a Motherless Child*
- *Summertime*
- *Take Five*
- *Three Ravens*
- *Tumbalalaika*
- *The Turtle Dove*
- *Wayfaring Stranger*
- *We Three Kings of Orient Are*
- *What Do You Do with a Drunken Sailor?*
- *When Jesus Wept*
- *When Johnny Comes Marching Home*
- *Winken, Blinken, and Nod*
- *Zum Gali Gali*

Variation 1

When you feel you can play through many familiar tunes by ear in all the minor keys with equal facility, begin again, this time taking more liberties with the basic tunes

1. Add ornaments.
2. Add connecting runs between chord tones.
3. Change registers, dynamics, meter, and/or timbre.
4. Jazz up the rhythms, and so on.

Variation 2

At the point where you feel you can play through many familiar tunes by ear in all the minor keys with equal facility, you could play through twelve tunes a day, playing each in a different minor key. Or, if you have time, play twenty-four, repeating the cycle twice.

Variation 3

After playing a tune in each key, spend an equal amount of time creating your own original minor tune, perhaps in the style of the tune you just played.

Variation 4

If the following list of familiar tunes isn't long enough or gets old, return to your favorite familiar tunes in major keys (most of them are) and change them to minor—by ear, of course, starting anew.

Key Switch

Play a major scale, up and down, one octave. Continue, adding the following wrinkles:

1. When turning around at the bottom, ascend with a different major scale. Example: descend in C, then ascend in E♭.
2. Do the same when turning around at the top. Example: Ascend in F, then descend in E.
3. Next, switch keys in the middle of the octave.
4. Switch keys at random points along the way.
5. Make the switch with after fewer and fewer notes until you can switch every three notes.

Ideas

1. With each new wrinkle, slow the tempo and then gradually increase speed as you gain fluency.
2. Try alternating various kinds of scales:
   a. Scales a half step away (C to B)
   b. Scales a whole step away (C to D)
   c. Scales some distance away (C to F♯)
   d. Move from flat key to flat key, sharp key to sharp key, or mixed (B♭ to D♭; E to A; E♭ to G, etc.).
   e. Mix in new types of scales, such as various kinds of minor scales.
   f. Later consider adding modes (Lydian), pentatonic, chromatic, augmented, diminished, and constructed (Lydian-Dominant) scales.
3. When you feel fluent in any of the above at a good tempo, start adding interesting rhythms, meters, rests, articulations, and timbre changes.
4. At some point, change the length of scale from an octave to other lengths, both shorter and longer. Later, alternate long and short turnarounds lengths and/or make the length a random choice each time.
5. Repeat the whole exercise using *arpeggios*.
   a. Start with triad. or 1–♭3–5).
   b. Later add extensions, such as seventh, ninth, or even eleventh chords.
   c. See Chapter 12 (Resources) for examples.
6. Add a partner at any point and play the game as a duet. Consider imaginative mixing, such as one player playing scales, the other arpeggios. And/or: one plays in 6/8, the other in 3/4.
7. Adding percussion is always a good idea.
8. Write all the keys on three-by-five-inch cards. Select cards at random and lay them in a row to make a key-switch map.

Key Switch: Familiar Tune

When you're a pro at playing Key Switch (above), pick the melody of a familiar tune and switch keys every eight bars.

Variation 1

Make it every four bars.

Variation 2

Make it every two bars.

Variation 3

Make it every bar.

Variation 4

Use only two keys, switching back and forth. Expand it to three, four, and more in subsequent passes.

Variation 5

Use the key cards as described above to lay out a key map. Play with a partner, and switch keys together when one player nods.

Why not?

Make up your own melody and repeat the above.

Glassy Arpeggios

Minimalist composers such as Philip Glass and Steve Reich repeat arpeggio patterns (usually a string of eighth or sixteenth notes—this is easier on some instruments than others) over and over, occasionally introducing small changes in the pattern.

1. Invent an interesting arpeggio pattern and repeat it. And repeat it. And repeat.
2. At some point—perhaps a minute or two or three later—change something (one note).
3. Keep going with the new pattern. Keep the tempo, keep your focus.
4. Continue in this manner until you are playing an entirely new arpeggio, or until it's time for dinner, which ever comes first.

7
Aural Games

Play It Again, Sam

1. Improvise a bit of music, anything from a short motif (three to four notes) to an entire phrase.
2. Immediately play it back as exactly as possible. If it is too long or complex to remember exactly, shorten and/or simplify it.
3. As this facility develops, gradually increase the complexity (change keys, move from tonal to atonal, change rhythm and/or meter) and length.

Car Karaoke

This game challenges your ear, your voice, and develops your aural understanding of harmony and voice leading. But most of all, it's a lot of fun. It can be played anywhere that you have a bit of privacy (commuting in a car is one possibility).

1. Put on a CD of tuneful music, preferably something that has strong personal appeal for you. (I often select 60s rock or folk-rock music for this purpose.)
2. Invent harmonizing parts by singing them—loudly!
3. Sing one part above the melody if possible, and two or even three below the melody in different registers.

8
Technique Games

Fanfare

1. Pick an arpeggio of any chord type (major, minor, augmented, diminished, etc.) in any key.
2. Play alone (or enlist a friend and play as a duet) using notes from the chord (which may include the seventh or ninth) in fanfare-style figures (duple, triple, or both in alternation).

Change That Etude

1. Play any technical exercise or pattern with which you are familiar (an example for brass players might be the Herbert L. Clarke cornet technique exercises).
2. Repeat in every minor key.

Spontaneous Loop

1. Pick a restriction (e.g., a C pentatonic major scale [scale degrees 1–2–3–5–6]) and start improvising.
2. At frequent intervals (i.e., whenever you play something interesting—melody, melodic motif, pattern, lick, etc.), loop it for a while until you can remember it and play it fluently. It's okay to slow it down a bit and loop and learn.
3. After you've spent a little time with the snippet, continue improvising and repeat the process.

Idea 1

At some point, see if you can remember what you worked on earlier (or even yesterday!). Repeat it and work on it again.

Idea 2

After an idea is looped to fluency, explore it further by adding variations (e.g., change a note), transposing it, adding decorations (grace notes, glisses, etc.), playing it in retrograde or inverting it, or by augmentation or diminution.

Variation

Repeat with two players, stealing as much from each other as possible.

Work-up Scales

1. Choose your least familiar scale of any type (major, minor, modal, etc.).

2. Restrict yourself to scale steps one and two.

3. Explore and experiment with all the ways you can go back and forth between the two notes, varying:

   a. tempo
   b. articulation
   c. note values
   d. dynamics
   e. timbre (extended techniques
   f. meter
   g. rests

4. After the pair seems very familiar, move on to scale steps two and three.

5. Continue diatonically up the scale in this manner.

6. Now begin anew, this time using three notes at a time, beginning with scale steps one, two, and three.

7. Discover all the ways you can move between these notes, first using adjacent notes, then introducing leaps.

8. Move up diatonically as before.

   a. This should all take a bit of time; don't rush it.

9. At this point you may either repeat the process in all other keys or continue the process in your chosen key using the first four notes of your scale and proceeding as described above. True gluttons for excellence will go on to five notes and more.

9
Style Games

Dirge

1. Create the saddest piece you can. Use these suggestions:

   a. minor keys
   b. extended techniques
   c. low register
   d. long tones
   e. dynamic contrasts
   f. dissonance
   g. slow tempo

2. Give it a name (as you do with all your pieces) and/or dedicate it to a dearly departed friend or relative.

Variation City

1. Play any familiar tune (see Chapter 12 for a list of familiar tunes) by heart in your most unfamiliar key.

2. Play successive repetitions in different styles, such as:

   a. March
   b. Waltz
   c. Lullaby
   d. Fanfare
   e. Tango
   f. Blues
   g. Polka
   h. Elegy
   i. Jig
   j. Boogie
   k. Zydeco
   l. Sarabande

   See Chapter 12 for a list of additional musical styles.

3. If you need to do a little listening or research to learn more about the style ("What is the characteristic rhythm of a sarabande?"), go right ahead.

Holiday Time

1. Invent music that illustrates a holiday. Examples:

   a. Create the fourth of July in music.
   b. Play spooky Halloween music (turn out the lights!).
   c. Make up music that captures the feeling of Christmas time.
   d. Make a musical valentine.
   e. Improvise music that depicts Thanksgiving from 1) the Pilgrims' point of view and 2) the turkey's point of view.

10
Texture Game

Motorvation

Every instrument, even those with relatively slow technique, has *some* kind of movement that can be done very quickly to give the impression of motion—if not often (or perhaps ever) asked for by composers. To right this wrong and avenge this neglect, very methodically explore and catalog all the possibilities on your instrument for creating fast motion—wiggle the keys, slide the fingers, doing whatever you have to do to be able to create a continuous sense of fast motion. Most often this will be some kind of up-and-back motion within a limited range. Explore this two ways:

1. As a sound effect without tonal center
2. As a series of notes that are distinctly in a key

For the latter, take some time to explore each of the twelve keys and see if and where (low, middle, and high ranges) and how you can create a motor motion. Come up with as many as you can in both categories.

When you've acquired something of a motor vocabulary, invent a piece that uses a lot of this effect. Perhaps give it an evocative title such as:

1. Waterfall
2. Indy 500
3. The Hive
4. Is that My Stomach?
5. B-52 Parade
6. Humming Along
7. Rat Race
8. My Harley

11
Miscellaneous Games

Daily Arkady

Russian hornist Arkady Shilkloper is one of the most creative musicians on the planet. When asked how he warms up, he simply says he "plays music," He investigates simultaneously music, technique, and his needs as a player. He finds a rhythmic or melodic fragment and follows it where it leads, mindful of what the current state of his embouchure needs to warm up.

I've given this procedure the name of the "Daily Arkady" in honor of this brilliant musician. A Daily Arkady is thus a refreshing and highly effective integration of technique and musicality, and is (or should be) a different type of adventure every time.

DAs may be focused in a certain area if desired. Examples:

1. Chords or chord progressions
2. Rhythms
3. Styles
4. Scales
5. Arpeggios
6. Extended techniques

However, most days the best idea is to be alert, aware, adventurous, and begin. Follow the line wherever it leads.

Tip

As with most of your improvising, you would do well to *record* what you play. You can decide afterwards if you wish to keep or erase your recording, but it would be a shame to produce some astonishingly beautiful or inventive spontaneous music that is lost forever. A DA will do that much more often than chance would allow.

You might also come up with something that you would like to polish into a composition later. So don't delay, record today!

Chord Hopping

Perhaps as part of a DA, fun and effective chord practice can be had by freely improvising back and forth between two chords. At first it may seem halting and full of hesitation. Stick with it until the movement feels automatic, familiar, and fluent. Any two chords will do.

Suggestions

1. Major chords a half step apart (C to D♭ or C to B)
2. Major chords a whole step apart (C to D or D to E)
3. Mix chord types (C—E♭m C—A♭7, and so on).

Tip

Try limiting play at first on each chord to:

1. Scales
2. Arpeggios
3. Short melodic patterns, like 1—2—3—1 (C—D—E—C in C major).
4. Mix several types at once.

Transposition Map

This is a good game to play after acquiring some proficiency with Chord Hopping (above).

1. Pick a short series of tones in a key. Example: 1—2—3—5 in C major.
2. Write down a series of (random) keys. Example: C, E♭, B, A, F♯, D, B♭, D♭, A♭, and G).
3. Play the tone series without pause through each key on the map you created.

Tip

If you hesitate at all when switching between any two chords, loop the two until the transition is smooth, effortless, and automatic.

Variation 1

Play the map backwards.

Variation 2

Try tone series using other scale types:

1. Minor
2. Dominant seventh
3. Diminished
4. Augmented
5. Whole-tone
6. Blues
7. Pentatonic
8. Etc.

Duet for One

Piano is highly suggested for this one (but it also works for guitar, strings, mallet percussion, etc.) (Source: Charles Young.)

1. Improvise on the piano and *sing* exactly the same line in unison.
2. Experiment with:
   a. Leaps
   b. Syncopations
   c. Repetition of motifs
   d. Other challenges.

Duet for One Revisited

1. Record some kind of accompaniment figure on your instrument or a percussion instrument for at least five minutes:
   a. Ostinato   d. Arpeggiated figure
   b. Long tones   e. Drone
   c. Bass line   f. Pulsed drone
2. Play back the recording and solo over it.

Idea

Save these homemade accompaniments and build a library of them. Later you can pick one out at any time for soloing over (saving the time of constructing one each time). But keep adding to them to keep your collection fresh.

Intervals

This games works best on piano, but may be played by other instruments as well.

1. Select your least familiar key.
2. Improvise an interesting melody line using only:
   a. Unisons or octaves (plus diatonic steps)
   b. Scale degrees 1 and 5
   c. Scale degrees 1, 4, and 5
   d. Scale degrees 1, 2, and 5
   e. Choice of the root of a chord or the tonic of the key) plus any two or three other notes
      1. In the major scale
      2. In the chromatic scale
3. Change octaves with any of these at will.
4. Players skilled at piano may assign the accompaniment function to one hand and solo with the other.
5. Repeat (perhaps revisiting daily), working your way through all keys.

Sequences

1. Decide on a simple one-measure pattern in a major key
2. Start with quarter and half notes only (the measure may be invented or selected from a current solo, etude, or orchestral/band excerpt).
3. Play the measure in diatonic sequence up one octave and down again.
4. Repeating it in all keys is a good idea.

Suggestion

Repeat in minor.

Drifting

1. Invent a simple melody in C major.
2. At some point, choose a common tone leading to a new key.
3. Continue in the new key.
4. Repeat the procedure *ad libitum*.

Examples

1. In the key of C major, E becomes the root of E major.
2. Then the B (fifth) of E major becomes the third of F♯ minor.
3. And so on.

Variation 1

Any scale step of the old key may be the common tone in the new key. Example: A, the sixth scale degree in C major becomes the fourth degree in E minor.

Variation 2

Same procedure as above, using arpeggios only.

Variation 3

Mix arpeggios and scales.

Makeover

1. Play any familiar tune or technical pattern in a major key.
2. Change from major to other kinds of scales, such as:

    a. Dominant seventh
    b. Whole tone
    c. Chromatic
    d. Diminished
    e. Altered
    f. Phrygian
    g. Lydian
    h. Blues scale

Suggesting Harmony (inspired by Charles Young)

1. Pick a simple chord progression (use V—I to start), time signature, and tempo.
2. Play several times through using arpeggios only
   a. Ascending
   b. Descending
   c. Both
3. Repeat, doing the same with scales.
4. Then play again, using both arpeggios and scales, always using them in such a way that the underlying chords are clear.

Suggestion

Use lots of chord tones, especially on strong beats.

Two-Five (iim^7–V^7)

1. Improvise freely in 4/4 over the iim^7—V^7 progressions listed below.

Dm^7—G^7	B♭m^7—E♭^{7}	F♯m^7—B^7
Gm^7—C^7	E♭m^7—A♭^{7}	Bm^7—E^7
Cm^7—F^7	A♭m^7—D♭^{7}	Em^7—A^7
Fm^7—B♭^{7}	C♯m^7—F♯^{7}	Am^7—D^7

2. At first, make the time spent on each chord indefinite before changing in order to acquire familiarity with getting around the chord:
   a. Scale-wise
   b. Arpeggios
   c. A mix of the two.
3. Change after a set number of measures of 4/4., (four, two, or one measure, or just two beats).
4. For each set number of measures, play the progression multiple times at different tempos.
   a. Start with a slow pulse and end with a brisk tempo.

Tips

1. A computer program such as *Band-in-a-Box* can provide a tireless accompaniment for you.
2. Take your time—it takes considerable time to be comfortable in each one of these.
3. Do them one at a time.
4. Don't go on to the next pair until each one is very familiar.
5. As you encounter each new pair, include a brief review of the keys already mastered.

Two-Five-One (iim^7–V^7–I)

Use the same instructions as in Two-Five above. The iim^7—V^7—I progression is the basis of most jazz standards.

The length of the iim^7—V^7 is commonly the same length as the I chord alone. Thus, in the key of C: if iim^7—V^7 (Dm^7—G^7) is one measure long, the resolution on I (C) is one measure long. If iim^7 (Dm^7) is one measure and V^7 (G^7) is one measure, then I (C) is two measures long.

Choose proportions and tempos that are comfortable to start with. Then gradually increase speed and decrease the length of time spent on each.

Over time, learn the iim^7—V^7—I progression in all keys.

Dm^7—G^7—C	B♭m^7—E♭^{7}—A♭	F♯m^7—B^7—E
Gm^7—C^7—F	E♭m^7—A♭^{7}—D♭	Bm^7—E^7—A
Cm^7—F^7—B♭	A♭m^7—D♭^{7}—G♭	Em^7—A^7—D
Fm^7—B♭^{7}—E♭	C♯m^7—F♯^{7}—B	Am^7—D^7—G

Something Blue

Using the Blues scale (1—2—♭3—♯4—5—♭7) in any key of your choice (in C: C—D—E♭—F♯—G—B♭), experiment with melodic and expressive possibilities. Mourn, complain, wail, whine, sob, cry out, tell a tale of regret, sorrow, and woe. Use rhythms and timbres of speech to enhance expression.

Daily Cadenza

Early in the day, right after your warm-ups, pick a piece in your repertoire that does *not* have a cadenza in it. Find a place near the end of it for a cadenza. Make one up! (Inspired by Eric Edberg)

Outside the Penta Box

One advantage in using pentatonic scales is that everything sounds great. The major pentatonic is spelled 1—2—3—5—6; the minor pentatonic is spelled 1—♭3—4—5—♭7 and is simply the sixth mode of the major pentatonic. It pays big dividends to be fluent in both of these, but you should also be aware of (and spend time in) other pentatonic scales. Examples:

Pelog	1—♭2—♭3—5—♭6
Hirajoshi	1—2—♭3—5—♭6
Kumoi	1—2—♭3—5—6

Create a piece that starts in major pentatonic and goes (upon a signal from one of the players) through all of these pentatonics and finally ends again in the major form. Over time become fluent in all keys.

Variations for pianists (Inspired by Vincent Persichetti[1])

1. The first time through this game, harmonize the melody with obvious diatonic chords.
2. Repeat using chords foreign to the key of the pentatonic scale, either occasionally or throughout.

---

1   *Twentieth Century Harmony.* NY: Norton, 1961, 50–52.

Substitution

For this one, you might need printed music.

1. Play any tune (familiar or unfamiliar, but a simple tune would be good to start with), but invent a new melody, using the rhythms of the original.

2. Stay in the same key, or go completely free or atonal.

Circling the Fifths

1. The material for this game may be:

    a. A motif or *short* melody snippet from any solo, etude, or repertoire excerpt on which you are currently working.

    b. Any basic unit of technique, such as a scale, triad (or rearranged triad), arpeggio, or pattern, in whole or in part.

    c. Any familiar tune or part thereof.

2. Simply play the selected melody successively through all keys, progressing downwards around the circle of fifths:

$$C—F—B\flat—E\flat—A\flat—D\flat—F\sharp/G\flat—B—E—A—D—G$$

This is a particularly useful order in which to acquire fluency, since each key has a dominant relationship to the next (C^7 to F^7 to $B\flat^7$, etc.).

This should be done daily as part of a technical review/development session. The goal is to embed basic technical activity deep into your musical DNA (muscle memory), so that when these basic units are encountered in the future, you must simply trigger or cue the sequence for it to flow easily rather than having to decipher the symbols visually and individually and then translate them into muscle activity. In the same way that you speak your own name, a well-learned bit of musical material is cued and produced effortlessly at will.

This exercise has the advantage of systematically acquiring the new material in all keys. *Memorize the circle of fifths as soon as possible, getting the knowledge off the paper and into you.*

Tip 1

Choose a tempo that ensures success. Tempo should normally start slow, gradually increasing with continued repetition and success.

Tip 2

Repeat the selected melody notes as many times per key as necessary to produce a feeling of confidence and relaxation. Any 'misses' provide evidence that you should slow down and increase the number of repetitions. For example, the first time through might mean playing the material without counting repetitions and staying in just one key or only a couple keys. Later, repeat the snippet eight, four, three, or two times, or ultimately just once per key before moving to the next.

Tip 3

Looping smaller groups of keys is very useful. Examples:

1. C—F
2. A♭—D♭
3. F♯—B
4. E♭—A♭—D♭
5. B—E—A
6. A♭—D♭—G♭—B
7. B—E—A—D

Tip 4

If a known melody (an excerpt or familiar tune) is used, play it using equal note values (e.g., all quarter notes) first before using the original rhythms. Ditto with articulation: play all staccato or legato before using the original.

Variation 1

Repeat in minor.

Variation 2

Try other kinds of scales, triads, and arpeggios (e.g., dominant seventh, diminished, augmented, modal).

Variation 3

Begin at another note than C.

Variation 4

Play backwards.

Variation 5

Add and vary articulation.

Variation 6

Play the snippet using different rhythmic ostinatos, such as: long-short-short, short-short-long, and short-long-short.

Variation 7

After the original basic form is well-learned, repeat, improvising articulations and note values along the way.

Variation 8

Repeat the tour of all keys, moving through them chromatically, either forwards or backwards, rather than following the circle of fifths

Scrambled Keys

1. Repeat Circling the Fifths above, but construct your own unpredictable row of keys. Examples:

   a. F♯—E—B♭—D—A♭—G—E♭—C—B—D♭—A—F

   b. A♭—C—D♭—A—B—G♭—F—D—E—B♭—G—E♭

2. Sample the variations suggested in Circling the Fifths.

Idea

Make up a new scrambled order every day.

Up-and-Down Sequences

It's a great skill to know how to outline the chords found in the major scale, especially by simply going up and down the scale. The simplest version of this would be a scale in thirds: 1—3—2—4—3—5, etc.

Extend that pattern to make it a triad, and you have a slightly more complex but very useful one that works well in triplets:

1. 1—3—5

   2—4—6

   3—5—7

   4—6—8

2. Etc.

3. Notation in C:

   etc.

   Notation as chords in C:

   etc.

5. For descending, invert triads (5—3—1).

6. Feel free to invent many patterns of this type, for example:

   a. Add a tone to the triad and make the pattern 1—2—3—5

   b. Double the third and make the pattern 1—3—5—3.

7. It will take time to acquire fluency in all keys, but the effort is well worth it.

Variation 1

Change direction of every other triad, which will make the line connect much more smoothly:

Variation 2

Repeat in the various minor scales.

Variation 3

Repeat in more exotic scales, such as:

1. Whole-tone
2. Diminished
3. Klezmer
4. Pentatonic major or minor

Arpeggio Progression

This is a quick way of generating a chord sequence.

1. Select a chord and arpeggiate it. The individual notes are the roots of each chord in the progression.
2. Start with major triads. Example: A C-major triad generates a progression of C—E—G.

3. Consider each note to be the tonic of a new key and improvise in the three keys: C major, E major, G major.
4. Experiment with different lengths of time per key, from a random or intuitive amount (which may be the same or different for each key), to various numbers of measures: sixteen, eight, four, two, one, or one-half.
5. Length of tune: cycle through the three keys until it seems like a good time to stop or Tuesday, whichever comes first.

Tip

There are two uses of chords that are easy to confuse:

1. The *generating chord* (there is only one of these).
2. The *progression chord*, which is built on a note of the generating chord (there is one of these for each note of the generating chord—three for a triad).

Example

1. Generating chord: C triad (C—E—G).
2. Progression chords: C major—E major—G major.

It is especially important to keep these straight as the generating chords become longer and the progression chords become more complex.

Idea 1

Repeat using generating triads in all keys.

Idea 2

Vary these musical elements:

1. Dynamics
2. Tempo
3. Timbre
4. Density
5. Rhythms
6. Articulation
7. Tessitura
8. Meter (including odd meters)

Idea 3

It's easier to play when you select a style, such as:

1. Baroque
2. Calypso
3. Waltz
4. March
5. Sci-fi soundtrack
6. Children's song
7. Samba
8. Fanfare
9. Renaissance
10. Zydeco
11. Etc.

Idea 4

Use the computer program *Band-in-a-Box* for accompaniment.

Idea 5

Sing it!

Variation: 1

Use minor triads for generating chords (e.g., C—E♭—G).

Variation 1

Use minor keys for progression chords.

Variation 2

Use a mix of major and minor chords for progression chords.

Variation 3

Try other kinds of three-note triads for both generating and progression chords. Examples:

1. Augmented (1—3—♯5)
2. Diminished (1—♭3—♭5)
3. Suspended (1—4—5, 1—2—5)

Variation 4
Mix and match all kinds of three-note triads for progression chords. Examples for C—E—G:

Variation 5
Use more complex chords on each key of the progression, (minor sevenths and ninths, major sevenths, etc.) Examples for a C-major generating chord:

Variation 6
1. Build longer progressions using four- and five-note chords instead of triads. Examples:
2. As before, you may assign any chord quality (major, minor, dominant seventh, augmented, diminished, half-diminished, etc.) to any of the chords in the progression.
3. Don't rush to make a long string as complex as possible too soon.
4. Spend much time becoming fluent at following the progression using simple chords (triads).
5. Over time, gradually increase the number of complex chords.

Connect the Dots
1. Choose a familiar tune that uses a limited number of basic (I—IV—V) chords, such as "Amazing Grace."
2. Once you are comfortable finding the melody in C major, play it again, this time filling in the notes between any leaps in the melody. These are ornamental (passing) notes, so they can be played quite quickly.
3. Repeat in all keys.

Suggestion (idea from Lori Warner)
When you are comfortable with the process, round up an accompanist who can play chords or bass (or one of each) while you play your decorated melody.

Variation 1
Repeat in minor.

Variation 2
Repeat the process in other familiar tunes.

Variation 3
Choose a new tune, this time one with more and more complex harmonies.

Arpeggio Alternation

1. Improvise using arpeggios only, going back and forth between two chords.
2. Use only three notes at first, staying as "level" as you can when moving to the new chord.
3. Play the notes first in order ascending, then descending, then mixed and/or alternating.
4. Then jumble the order each time.
5. Vary the tempo, articulation rhythms, and/or dynamics.
6. Over time, try in all registers.

Suggestion

Start with a pair of keys that follow the circle of fifths (descending; each is the dominant of the following key):

C—F—B♭—E♭—A♭—D♭—G♭/F♯—B—E—A—D—G

Examples

1. C to F: C—E—G—C—F—A (The second chord is in second inversion to keep the notes at approximately the same pitch level with the first arpeggio.)
2. Another version of C to F: C—E—G—A—F—C or C—E—G—F—C—A (Sometimes there are two equal choices. Try them both!)

Idea 1

Keep Chord 1 the same while changing Chord 2 until you've gone through the whole cycle.

Idea 2

1. First move from major chord to major chord.
2. Then try:
   a. Minor to minor
   b. Major to minor
      ͻr to major
3. Later, try:
   a. Dominant seventh
   b. Diminished
   c. Augmented

Variation 1

Use four-note chords.

Variation 2

Use more than four chord notes per arpeggio. Example:

C—E—G—B♭—D (C^9)

Variation 3

Try other orders of key progression, such as:

1. Chromatic (C—D♭—D, etc.)
2. Whole tone (C—D—E)
3. Major diatonic (C—Dm—Em—F—G^7, etc.)
4. Common chord progressions (I—iiim^7—vi^7—iim^7—V^7; I—IV—V^7)
5. Uncommon chord progressions (C—F♯ minor—B♭^{7}—E—A+—D♭m)

12
Patterns and Scales

Cycles

All scales and patterns can be practiced descending as well as ascending, and can be practiced ascending/descending in alternation in cycles or diatonic progression. Patterns can be combined as well (1—2—3—4, 5—3—2—1).

C—F—Bb—Eb—Ab—Db—Gb/F#—B—E—A—D—G

C—G—D—A—E—B—F#/Gb—Db—Ab—Eb—Bb—F

C—F—G—Bb—D—Eb—A—Ab—E—Db—B—Gb

C—Db—D—Eb—E—F—F#/Gb—G—Ab—A—Bb—B

C—B—Bb—A—Ab—G—Gb/F#—F—E—Eb—D—Db

C—D—E—F#—Ab—Bb—Db—Eb—F—G—A—B

C—Bb—Ab—Gb—E—D—Db—B—A—G—F—Eb

C—B—A—G—F—Eb—Db—Bb—Ab—Gb/F#—E—D

C—F#—Db—G—D—Ab—Eb—A—E—Bb—F—B

C—Gb—D—F—Bb—E—A—Eb—Ab—D—G—Db

C—Db—B—D—Bb—Eb—A—E—Ab—F—G—F#

C—Eb—F#—A—B—D—F—Ab—Bb—Db—E—G

C—A—F#—Eb—B—Ab—F—D—Bb—G—E—C#

C—E—G—Bb—Ab—F—B—D—Eb—F#—A—Db

C—A—F—E—Bb—A—G—Eb—B—Db—D—Gb

Bb—A—C—B—Ab—D—F—G—E—Db—Eb—F#

Major Patterns

1—2—3—4—5—6—7
1—7—1
1—2—3
1—2—3—4
1—2—3—4—5
1—2—3—5
1—2—3—5—6
     (pentatonic major; variation: ♭6)

1—2—3—5—7
1—2—3—5—7—9
1—3—4—5
1—3—5—(8)
1—3—5—6
1—3—5—7
1—3—5—7—9
1—2—4—5

Dominant Seventh Patterns

Scale: 1—2—3—4—5—6—♭7
1—3—5—♭7
1—2—3—5—♭7
1—3—5—♭7—9
1—3—5—♭7—♯9—♭9 (8)

Whole-tone Patterns

Scale: 1—2—3—♯4—♯5—♭7
1—2—3—♯4—♯5
1—2—3—♯5
1—3—♯5
1—3—♯5—♭7

Minor Patterns

1—2—♭3
1—2—♭3—4—5
1—2—♭3—4—5—(♭)6
1—2—♭3—5
1—2—♭3—5—♭7
1—2—♭3—5—♭7—9
1—♭3—4—5
1—♭3—4—5—♭7 (minor pentatonic)
1—♭3—5
1—♭3—5—6
1—♭3—5—♭7 (or ♮7)
1—♭3—5—♭7—9

Diminished Patterns

1—2—♭3—4—♭5—♭6—♭♭7—7 (whole-half)
1—b2—♭3—3—♯4—5—6—♭7 (half-whole)
1—♭3—♭5

1—♭3—♭5—6 (♭♭7 equals 6 here)
1—2—♭3—♭5
1—2—♭3—4—♭5

Additional Scales from Which to Extract Patterns

Dorian	1—2—♭3—4—5—6—♭7	Klezmer 1 (Ahava Raba)	1—♭2—3—4—5—♭6—♭7
Phrygian	1—♭2—♭3—4—5—♭6—♭7	Klezmer 2 (Misheberekh)	1—2—♭3—♯4—5—6—♭7
Spanish Phrygian	1—♭2—3—4—5—♭6—♭7	Jazz melodic minor	1—2—♭3—4—5—6—7
Lydian	1—2—3—♯4—5—6—7		(both directions)
Mixolydian	1—2—3—4—5—6—♭7	Harmonic minor	♭6—♮7
Aeolian	1—2—♭3—4—5—♭6—♭7	Arpeggiation of chords	3—5—1 (down one octave:
Locrian	1—2—♭3—4—♭5—♭6—♭7		3—5—1)
Superlocrian	1—♭2—♭3—♭4—♭5—♭6—♭7	Pentatonic	1—2 (down one octave)—
Lydian Dominant	1—2—3—♯4—5—6—♭7		6—1—5—6—3—5—2—
Chromatic	Fluency from any note to any note		3—1 (and ascending)
Blues	1—♭3—4—♯4—5—♭7		

Intervals

Scales in thirds

Scales in fourths

Variations and extensions:

$\quad$ 1—4—$\flat$7

$\quad$ 1—4—5 (1)

$\quad$ 1—4—5—$\flat$7—1

Leap from the tonic to all other notes, both diatonically and chromatically as well as ascending and descending.

Any interval through all keys, both ascending and descending.

Approach Note Patterns

Add a chromatic or diatonic approach notes to arpeggios and patterns.

Chord Progression (iim^7–V^7–I)

Dm7—G7—C	Abm7—D$\flat$7—G$\flat$
Gm7—C7—F	C$\sharp$m7—F$\sharp$7—B
Cm7—F7—B$\flat$	F$\sharp$m7—B7—E
Fm7—B$\flat$7—E$\flat$	Bm7—E7—A
B$\flat$m7—E$\flat$7—A$\flat$	Em7—A7—D
E$\flat$m7—A$\flat$7—D$\flat$	Am7—D7—G

13
Familiar Tunes

The Beatles
All My Loving
All You Need Is Love
And I Love Her
Can't Buy Me Love
A Day in the Life
Eleanor Rigby
A Hard Day's Night
Here Comes the Sun
Hey Jude
I Call Your Name
I Saw Her Standing There
I Wanna Hold Your Hand
I Will
I'm a Loser
In My Life
Lady Madonna
Let It Be
Maxwell's Silver Hammer
Michelle
Norwegian Wood
Ob-La-Di, Ob-La-Da
Penny Lane
Sgt. Pepper's Lonely Hearts Club Band
She Loves You
Ticket to Ride
When I'm Sixty-Four
With a Little Help from My Friends
Yellow Submarine

Bossa Nova
Blue Bossa
Corcavado
Desafinado
Girl from Ipanema
Meditation
One Note Samba
Wave

British, Irish, and Scottish
All through the Night
Annie Laurie
The Ash Grove
Auld Lang Syne
Barbara Allen
The Blue Bells of Scotland
Cockles and Mussels
Danny Boy
Down by the Sally Gardens
Flow Gently Sweet Afton
Foggy, Foggy Dew
The Girl I Left Behind Me
Greensleeves
The Gypsy Rover
Ilkla Moor Bhat Hat
Irish Washerwoman
It's a Long Way to Tipperary
John Peel
The Keel Row
The Keeper
Loch Lomond
Londonderry Air
Lord Randall
The Minstrel Boy
My Wild Irish Rose
The Night That Paddy Murphy Died
Oh, No, John!
The Rakes of Mallow
Rule, Brittania
Scarborough Fair
Skye Boat Song
Three Ravens
The Turtle Dove
The Wearing of the Green
When Irish Eyes Are Smiling
Whiskey in the Jar
Ye Banks and Braes

Broadway/Movies

America (from *West Side Story*)
Camelot
Do, Re, Mi
Don't Cry for Me, Argentina
Edelweiss
Food, Glorious Food
Getting to Know You
Give My Regards to Broadway
Hey, Look Me Over
I Could Have Danced all Night
I Feel Pretty
If Ever I Would Leave You
If I Were a Rich Man
The Impossible Dream
Maria
Master of the House
Moon River
My Favorite Things
New York, New York
O What a Beautiful Mornin'
Oklahoma!
Over the Rainbow
Send in the Clowns
Seventy-six Trombones
Somewhere
Soon It's Gonna Rain
Sunrise, Sunset
The Surrey with the Fringe on Top
Tea for Two
Tonight
With a Little Bit of Luck
Wouldn't It Be Lovely?

Children's Songs

A-Hunting We Will Go
A Tisket, a-Tasket
All the Pretty Little Horses
Alphabet Song
Animal Fair
Baa, Baa, Black Sheep
Baby Beluga
The Bear Went over the Mountain
Big Rock Candy Mountain
Bingo (B-I-N-G-O)
Bye Baby Bunting
Do Your Ears Hang Low?

Eensy Weensy Spider
The Farmer in the Dell
Go Tell Aunt Rhody
Goober Peas
Good Morning, Merry Sunshine
Hokey Pokey
Hot Cross Buns
Hush, Little Baby
I've Got Sixpence
John Jacob Jingleheimer Schmidt
Lightly Row
London Bridge
Mary Had a Little Lamb
Michael Finnegan
Muffin Man
Mulberry Bush
My Hat, It Has Three Corners
Oats, Peas, Beans, and Barley Grow
Old Gray Mare
Old Joe Clark
Old King Cole
Old Macdonald
Polly Wolly Doodle
Pop Goes the Weasel
Rain, Rain, Go Away
Ring Around the Rosies
Rock-a-Bye Baby
Rubber Ducky
Sarasponda
She'll Be Comin' Round the Mountain
Sing a Song of Sixpence
Sippin' Cider through a Straw
Skip to My Lou
Take Me Out to the Ball Game
There's a Hole in the Bucket
This Old Man
Tom, Tom, the Piper's Son
Twinkle, Twinkle, Little Star
The Wheels on the Bus
Winken, Blinken, and Nod

Classical

Anvil Chorus
Ave Maria
Barcarolle
The Blue Danube
Brahm's Lullaby
Bridal Chorus (Lohengrin)

Can-Can
Carnival of Venice
The Dance of the Hours
Dies Irae
Eine Kleine Nachtmusik
The Fledermaus Waltz
Funeral March (Chopin)
Für Elise
Habanera
The Hall of the Mountain King
Hallelujah Chorus
Humoresque
Hunter's Chorus (Freischütz)
It Was a Lover and His Lass
La Che Darem La Mano
La Donna È Mobile
Light Cavalry Overture
The New World Symphony
Ode to Joy
Peter and the Wolf
Pilgrim's Chorus
Polyvetsian Dances
Pomp and Circumstance
Sumer Is Icumen In
The Surprise Symphony
Tales from the Vienna Woods
Triumphal March (Aida)
Trumpet Voluntary
Una Voce Poco Fa
Water Music
Wedding March (from *Lohengrin*)
Wedding March (Mendelssohn)
William Tell Overture

Contemporary Oldies
America (Paul Simon)
American Pie
Both Sides Now
Bridge over Troubled Waters
California Dreamin'
Country Roads
The Last Thing on My Mind
Long Black Veil
Mr. Bojangles
Mrs. Robinson
The Night They Drove Old Dixie Down
Pack up Your Sorrows
Puff the Magic Dragon

Ramblin' Boy
Sounds of Silence
Teach Your Children
Thirsty Boots
The Times They Are a-Changin'
The Weight
Where Have all the Flowers Gone?

Folk Songs
Abide with Me
Arkansas Traveler
Aura Lee
Billy Boy
Blue Tail Fly
Buffalo Gals
Camptown Races
Careless Love
Casey Jones
Cindy
Clementine
The Crawdad Song
Darlin' Corey
Day-O
Dixie
Down in the Valley
Erie Canal
The Flying Trapeze
Follow the Drinking Gourd
For He's a Jolly Good Fellow
Frankie and Johnny
Freight Train
Froggie Went a-Courtin'
Good Night, Ladies
Goodbye Old Paint
Grandfather's Clock
Green Grow the Lilacs
Hail, Hail, the Gang's all Here
Home on the Range
I Gave My Love a Cherry
I Ride an Old Paint
I'm Forever Blowing Bubbles
I've Been Working on the Railroad
Irene, Good Night
It Ain't Gonna Rain no More
Jimmy Crack Corn
John Henry
Kookaburra
Landlord, Fill the Flowing Bowl

Listen to the Mockingbird
The Little Brown Jug
Liza Jane
Long, Long Ago
Mountain Dew
My Bonnie
My Love Is Like a Red, Red Rose
Oh, Dear, What Can the Matter Be?
Oh, Susanna
Oh, Them Golden Slippers
Old Chisholm Trail
Old Dan Tucker
Old Rosin the Beau
On Top of Old Smoky
Peg O' My Heart
Pick a Bale of Cotton
Red River Valley
The Riddle Song
Rock 'O My Soul
Salty Dog
Shenandoah
Shoo Fly
Shortnin' Bread
Simple Gifts
St. James Infirmary
Stagger Lee
Stewball
The Streets of Laredo
Swanee River
Sweet Betsy from Pike
Ta-Ra-Ra Boom-Di-Ay
The Entertainer (Rag)
There Is a Tavern in the Town
Today
Tom Dooley
Tom, Tom, the Piper's Son
Turkey in the Straw
Wabash Cannonball
Wait for the Wagon
Waltzing Matilda
The Water Is Wide
When Irish Eyes Are Smilin'
Wiffenpoof Song
The Worried Man Blues
Yellow Bird
The Yellow Rose of Texas
You Are My Sunshine

Foreign Language
Alouette
Au Clair De La Lune
Aupres De Ma Blonde
Cielito Lindo
Frere Jacques
Funiculi Funicula
Gaudeamus Igitur
Guantanamera
Hava Nagila
La Bamba
La Cucaracha
La Marseillaise
Moscow Nights
Plaisir D'amour
Sakura
Santa Lucia
Sur Le Pont D'avignon
Tumbalalaika
Vive L'amour
Zum Gali Gali

George Gershwin
Embraceable You
Fascinatin' Rhythm
A Foggy Day
I Got Rhythm
Lady Be Good
Let's Call the Whole Thing Off
The Man That I Love
Nice Work If You Can Get It
Of Thee I Sing
S'wonderful
Someone to Watch over Me
Summertime
They Can't Take That Away from Me

Holiday
Angels We Have Heard on High
Auld Lang Syne
Ave Maria
Bring a Torch, Jeanette Isabella
Deck the Halls
Dreydl, Dreydl
The First Noel
God Rest You Merry, Gentlemen
Good King Wenceslas

Hark! the Herald Angels Sing
Here We Come a-Wassailing
I Saw Three Ships
It Came Upon a Midnight Clear
Jingle Bells
Joy to the World
Little Drummer Boy
O Come Emmanuel
O *Du Fröhliche*
O Holy Night
O Little Town of Bethlehem
O Tannenbaum
Oh Come, all Ye Faithful
Rudolph the Red-nosed Reindeer
Silent Night
The Twelve Days of Christmas
The Wassail Song
We Three Kings of Orient Are
We Wish You a Merry Christmas
What Child Is This?
White Christmas

Jazz Standards
Ain't Misbehavin'
All of Me
All the Things You Are
Angel Eyes
Autumn Leaves
Bewitched
Blue Bossa
Blue Monk
Body and Soul
Caravan
Cherokee
The Days of Wine and Roses
Georgia on My Mind
Green Dolphin Street
How High the Moon
In the Mood
It Don't Mean a Thing…
The Look of Love
Misty
Mood Indigo
My Funny Valentine
Night and Day
Out of Nowhere
Satin Doll
The Shadow of Your Smile

Stella by Starlight
Sweet Georgia Brown
Take Five
Take the 'A' Train

Love Songs
Careless Love
Clementine
Down in the Valley
Every Night When the Sun Goes In
On Top of Old Smoky
Scarborough Fair
Sittin' on Top of the World
Tennessee Waltz

Marches
Entry of the Gladiators
The Stars and Stripes Forever
Washington Post March

Miscellaneous
Happy Birthday

Oldies But Goodies
Alexander's Ragtime Band
Beautiful Dreamer
The Beer Barrel Polka
A Bicycle Built for Two
Bill Bailey
Camptown Races
Grandfather's Clock
Hot Time in the Old Town Tonight
I Want a Girl (Just Like the Girl)
In the Evening by the Moonlight
K-K-K-Katy
Long, Long Ago
The Man on the Flying Trapeze
Oh, Susanna!
Old Folks At Home
Old Oaken Bucket
Sentimental Journey
The Sidewalks of New York

Patriotic
America the Beautiful
Battle Hymn of the Republic
The Caissons Song
Columbia, the Gem of the Ocean

God Bless America
Hail, Columbia
The Marines' Hymn
My Country, 'Tis of Thee
The Star-Spangled Banner
This Land Is Your Land
When Johnny Comes Marching Home
Yankee Doodle
You're a Grand Old Flag

Rock 'n' Roll

Barbara Ann
Bye-Bye Love
Goody, Goody
Hit the Road, Jack
Johnny B. Good
Love Potion Number Nine
Peggy Sue
Rock Around the Clock
Rockin' Robin

Rounds

Dona Nobis Pacem
Frere Jacques
Heigh Ho
Kookaburra
Little Tommy Tinker
Row, Row, Row Your Boat
Scotland's Burning
The Tallis Canon
Three Blind Mice
Why Shouldn't My Goose

Sea Shanties

A-Roving
Barnacle Bill
Blow the Man Down
Golden Vanity
Haul Away, Joe
What Do You Do with a Drunken Sailor?

Spirituals, Gospel Songs, and Hymns

A Mighty Fortress
Ain't Gonna Grieve My Lord No More
Amazing Grace
There Is a Balm in Gilead
Deep River
Do, Lord
Down by the Riverside
Ezekiel Saw the Wheel
Go Down, Moses
Go Tell It on the Mountain
He's Got the Whole World in His Hands
Jacob's Ladder
Joshua Fit the Battle of Jericho
Kum Ba Yah
Michael, Row the Boat Ashore
Oh Mary, Don't You Weep
Old-Time Religion
Rock of Ages
Rock-a My Soul
Steal Away
Sometimes I Feel Like a Motherless Child
Swing Low, Sweet Chariot
Wayfaring Stranger
When Jesus Wept
When the Saints Go Marching In
Will the Circle Be Unbroken

Waltzes

Anniversary Waltz
Blue Danube
Merry Widow Waltz
Tales of the Vienna Woods
Tennessee Waltz

Wiener Blut (Vienna Blood)

14
Styles and Forms

A
Adagio
Advertising jingle
Afro-cuban
Air
Aleatoric
Allemande
Ambient
Americana
Anthem
Antiphonal
Arabesque
Aria
Art song
Asian music
Atonal
Avant-garde

B
Bagatelle
Ballad
Ballroom dance
Barbershop quartet
Barcarolle
Baroque
Bebop
Beguine
Bel canto
Belly dance
Berceuse
Bluegrass
Blues
Bolero
Boogie-woogie
Bossa nova
Bourée

Brazilian jazz
Break dancing
British folk music
Broadway
Bulgarian folk
Butoh

C
Cabaret
Cachucha
Cajun
Cakewalk
Calypso
Can-can
Canon
Cantata
Canzona
Caprice
Carol
Celtic
Cha-cha
Chaconne
Chance music
Chanson
Chant
Charleston
Children's song
Chinese music
Choral prelude
Chorale
Circus music
Comic opera
Computer music
Concerto
Concerto grosso
Conductus

Contredanse
Cool jazz
Cossack dance
Counterpoint
Country folk
Country rock
Country western
Cowboy
Cumbia
Czardas

D
Dance music
Descant
Dirge
Dodecaphony
Drone

E
Early music
Easy listening
Electronic
Elegy
English madrigal
English music hall
Étude
Euro pop

F
Fandango
Fanfare
Farandole
Fight song
Film music
Flamenco
Folk music

Foxtrot
Fugue
Funeral music
Funk
Fusion

G
Gamelan
Gansta rap
Gavotte
Girl group
Gospel
Graduation music
Greek music
Gregorian chant
Grunge
Gypsy

H
Habanera
Halloween music
Hard rock
Hawaiian/hula
Highland fling
Hillbilly
Hip-hop
Hoedown
Honky-tonk
Hopak
Hora
Hornpipe
Horror music
Hunting music
Hymn

I

Impressionist
Impromptu
Intermezzo
Isorhythm

J

Japanese
Jazz
Jig
Jive
John Cage's music
Jug band

K

Klezmer

L

Ländler
Lied/lieder
Line dance
Lounge music
Love song
Lullaby

M

Madrigal
Mambo
March
Masque
Mass
Mazurka
Medieval music
Meditation music
Merengue
Mexican
Microtonal
Minimalism
Minnesang
Minuet
Mood music
Morris dance
Motet
Motown
Musette

Music concrète
Music hall
Musical theater
Muzak

N

Nashville sound
Neoclassical
New age
New Orleans jazz
Nocturne
Noise

O

Odd meter
Ode
Opera
Operetta
Oratorio
Ostinato
Overture

P

Partita
Paso doble
Passacaglia
Pastorale
Pavane
Pentatonic
Perpetual motion
Polka
Polonaise
Pop
Postmodern
Program music
Psychedelic
Punk rock

Q

Quadrille

R

Raga
Ragtime
Rain dance
Rap

Recitative
Reel
Reggae
Renaissance
Requiem
Rhapsody
Rhythm and blues
Riff
Rock
Rock 'n' roll
Rockabilly
Romance
Romantic
Rondo
Round
Rumba

S

Salsa
Saltarello
Samba
Sarabande
Scherzo
Schottische
Sea chantey
Serenade
Serial
Shimmy
Shuffle
Singspiel
Ska
Skiffle
Soft rock
Son montuno
Sonata
Song
Soul
Sound collage
Spiritual
Spoken word
Square dance
Stabat mater
Stephen foster
Stile antico
Strathspey
Stride

Striptease
Surf music
Swing
Symphonic
Syrto

T

Tango
Tap dance
Tarantella
Te deum
Techno
Tejano
Theme and variations
Third stream
Threnody
Tibetan
Tin Pan Alley
Toccata
Tone poem
Tribal
Trio sonata
Troubadours
Trouveres
Tuvan throat-singing
Twelve-tone

V

Vamp
Variation
Vaudeville
Virelais
Virginia reel

W

Waltz
War dance
Watusi
Wedding music
Western swing
Work song
World music

Y

Yodeling

Z

Zydeco

15
Alphabetical Index of Games

About the Author

With his broad range of musical interests and abilities, **Jeffrey Agrell** is a "hornist for all seasons." As a performer/educator he has played and taught the full gamut of horn literature, including the repertoire for symphony orchestra, opera, musicals, ballet, operetta, and solo and chamber music, while stretching personal artistic boundaries beyond the orchestra as a composer, writer, clinician, recording artist, and solo performer.

Besides performing, Agrell has always been interested in the creative process as evidenced in his longtime activities as a writer and a composer. He was on the editorial staffs of *The Horn Call* and the *Brass Bulletin* for many years and has over ninety published articles to his credit. As a composer he has written many commissions for professional chamber music ensembles. His *Rhythm Suite for Clarinet and Marimba* won First Prize in the 2000 composition contest of the International Clarinet Association. Many of Agrell's works have appeared on CD and have been broadcast on radio and television nationally and internationally.

Besides teaching standard horn repertoire, Agrell has been very interested in the expansion of technique and musicality offered by (non-jazz) improvisation, and he teaches a unique semester course in improvisation designed for classical musicians.

His book, *Improvisation Games for Classical Musicians*, was released in December 2007 by GIA Publications, Inc.